Simply Rock 50s

22 Rockin' Hits of the 1950s

Arranged by Dan Coates

D1305978

Simply Rock 50s is a collection of some of the greatest songs from one of the most pivotal decades in music history. These selections have been carefully arranged by Dan Coates for Easy Piano, making them accessible to pianists of all ages. Phrase markings, articulations, fingering, pedaling and dynamics have been included to aid with interpretation, and a large print size makes the notation easy to read.

Amidst great social change—such as the beginning of the desegregation movement and the emergence of the "teenager" as a social class—rock 'n' roll flourished in the 1950s. Deeply rooted in a multitude of American music genres (big band, bluegrass, and gospel, to name a few) and embraced by a wide diversity of musicians, rock 'n' roll liberated teenagers from the music of their parents' generation. Personalities like Jerry Lee Lewis ("Great Balls of Fire") and Fats Domino ("Blueberry Hill" and "I'm Walkin'") dazzled audiences with their captivating piano playing, while successful groups, including The Penguins ("Earth Angel"), The Bobbettes ("Mr. Lee"), and Dion and The Belmonts ("A Teenager In Love"), shined with doo-wop vocals. Teen idols like Eddie Cochran ("Summertime Blues") and Bobby Darin ("Splish Splash") performed for sold-out concerts and had fans glued to the radio. All of this music has influenced generations of musicians and has entertained audiences, young and old, around the world. For these reasons and more, the hits on the following pages are exciting to explore.

After all, this is Simply Rock 50s!

Music Plus ♩
Kitchener, Ont., Canada
1-800-608-5205
info@musicpluscorp.com

Alfred

Contents

Ain't That a Shame

Words and Music by
Antoine Domino and Dave Bartholomew
Arranged by Dan Coates

You're the one to blame.

So long,

Blueberry Hill

Words and Music by
Al Lewis, Vincent Rose and Larry Stock
Arranged by Dan Coates

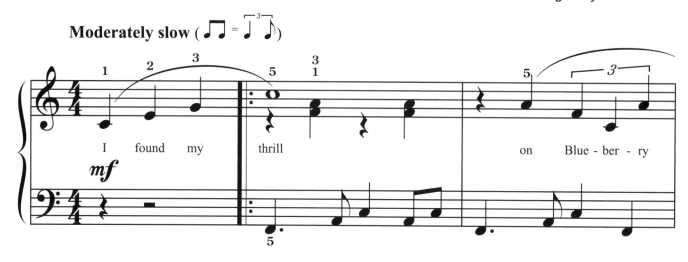

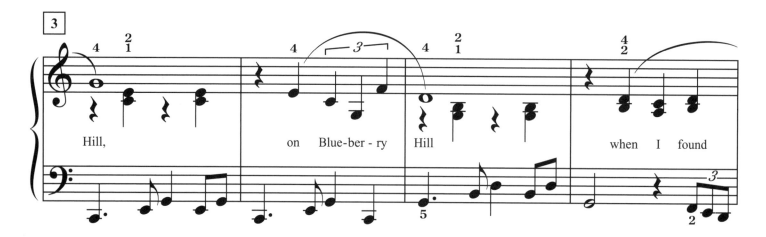

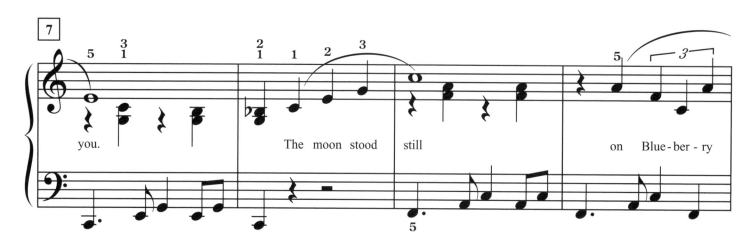

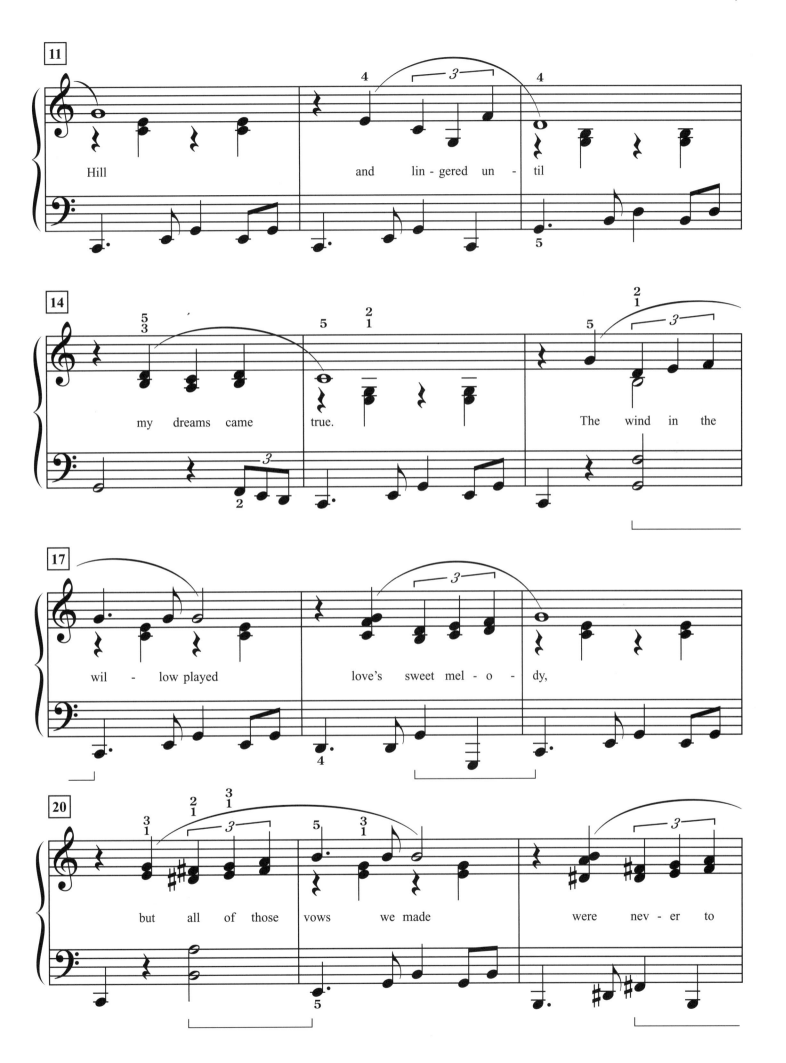

Chantilly Lace

Words and Music by J.P. Richardson
Arranged by Dan Coates

10

24

Ain't noth-in' in the world like a big-eyed girl___ that make me

mf

27

act so fun-ny, make me spend my mon-ey, make me feel real loose like a

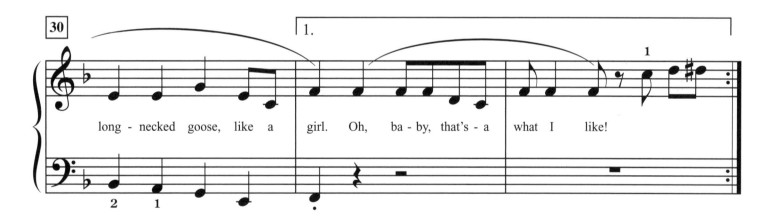

30

long-necked goose, like a girl. Oh, ba-by, that's-a what I like!

1.

33

2.

girl. Oh, ba-by, that's-a what I like!

Do You Want to Dance

Words and Music by Robert Freeman
Arranged by Dan Coates

Earth Angel
(Will You Be Mine)

Words and Music by Jesse Belvin
Arranged by Dan Coates

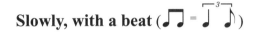

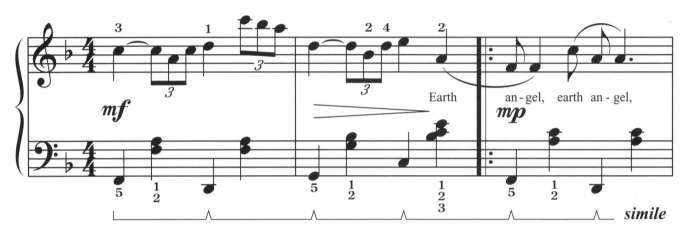

Earth an - gel, earth an - gel, the one I a - dore,___

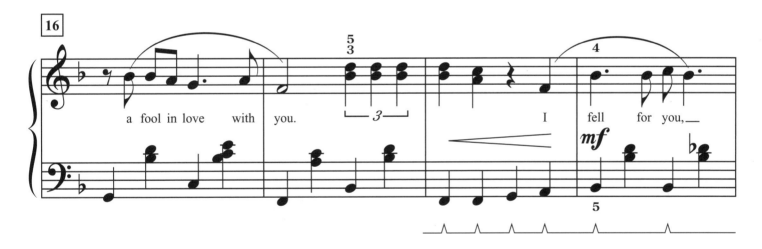

love you for - ev - er___ and ev - er more.___ I'm just a fool,_____

a fool in love with you. I fell for you,___

and I knew the vi - sion of your love's love-li - ness.___ I hope___ and I pray___

I'm Walkin'

Words and Music by
Antoine Domino and Dave Bartholomew
Arranged by Dan Coates

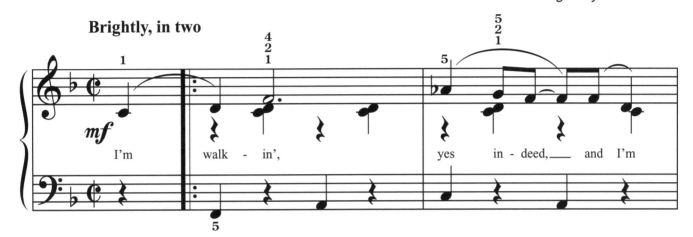

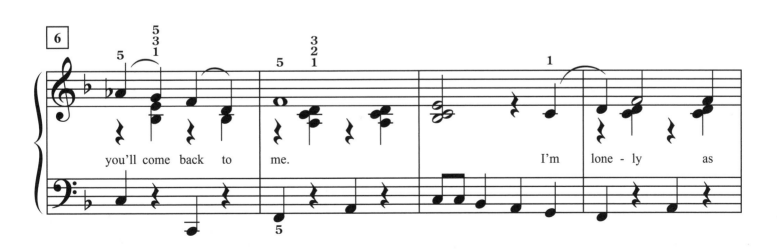

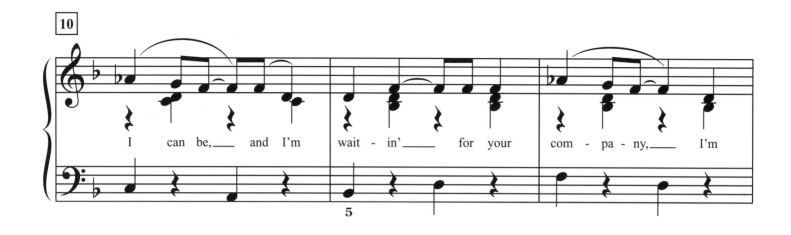

Great Balls of Fire

Words and Music by
Otis Blackwell and Jack Hammer
Arranged by Dan Coates

Brightly, with a rock beat

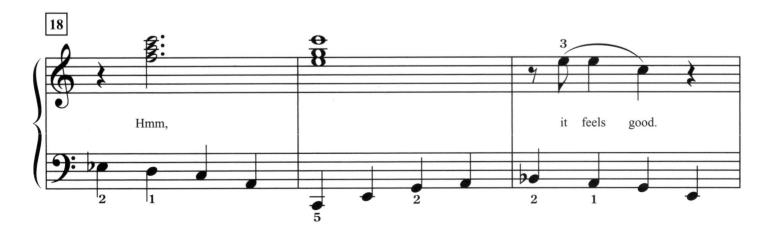

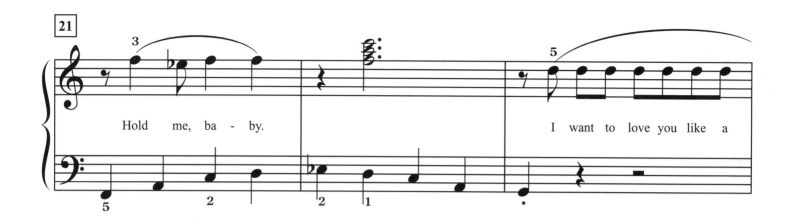

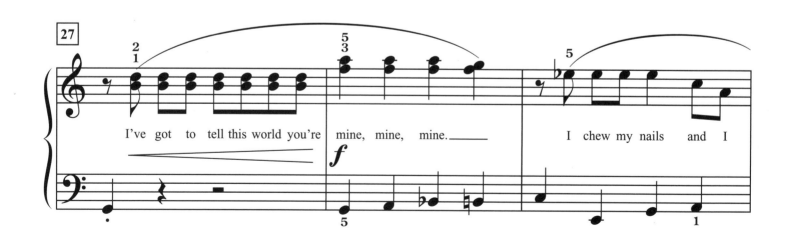

twid - dle my thumbs.___ I'm real ner - vous, but it sure is fun.___

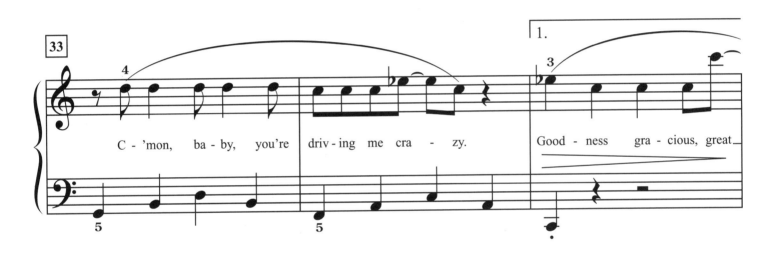

C - 'mon, ba - by, you're driv - ing me cra - zy. Good - ness gra - cious, great___

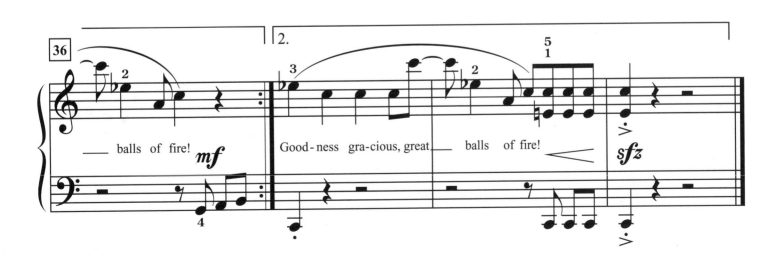

___ balls of fire! *mf* Good - ness gra-cious, great___ balls of fire! *sfz*

Hold Me, Thrill Me, Kiss Me

Words and Music by Harry Noble
Arranged by Dan Coates

Let the Good Times Roll

Words and Music by
Leonard Lee and Shirley Goodman
Arranged by Dan Coates

Lipstick on Your Collar

Words by Edna Lewis
Music by George Goehring
Arranged by Dan Coates

Mr. Lee

Words and Music by
Heather E. Dixon, Helen Gathers, Janice Pought,
Laura E. Webb and Emma Ruth Pought
Arranged by Dan Coates

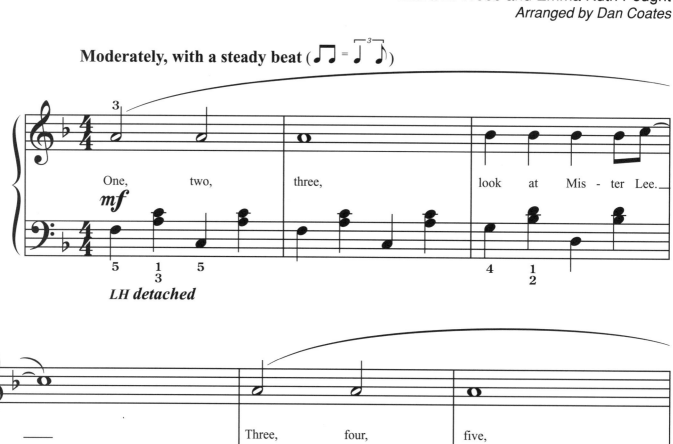

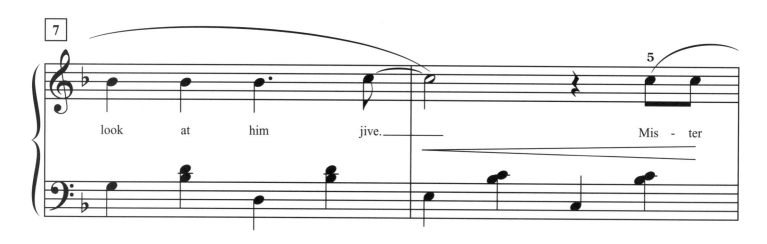

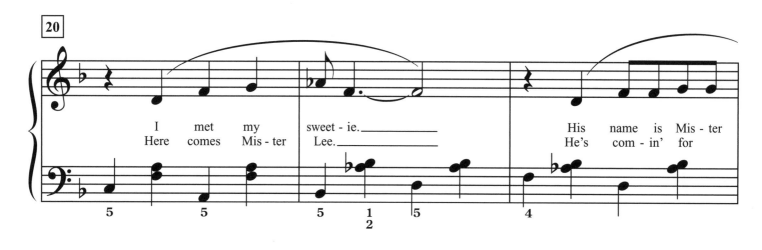

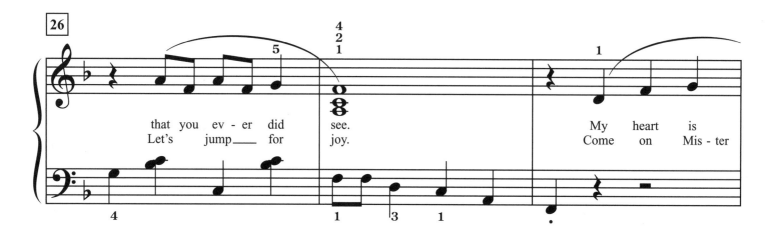

(We're Gonna) Rock Around the Clock

Words and Music by
Max C. Freedman and Jimmy DeKnight
Arranged by Dan Coates

A Rockin' Good Way
(To Mess Around and Fall In Love)

Words and Music by
Clyde Otis, Brook Benton and Luchi DeJesus
Arranged by Dan Coates

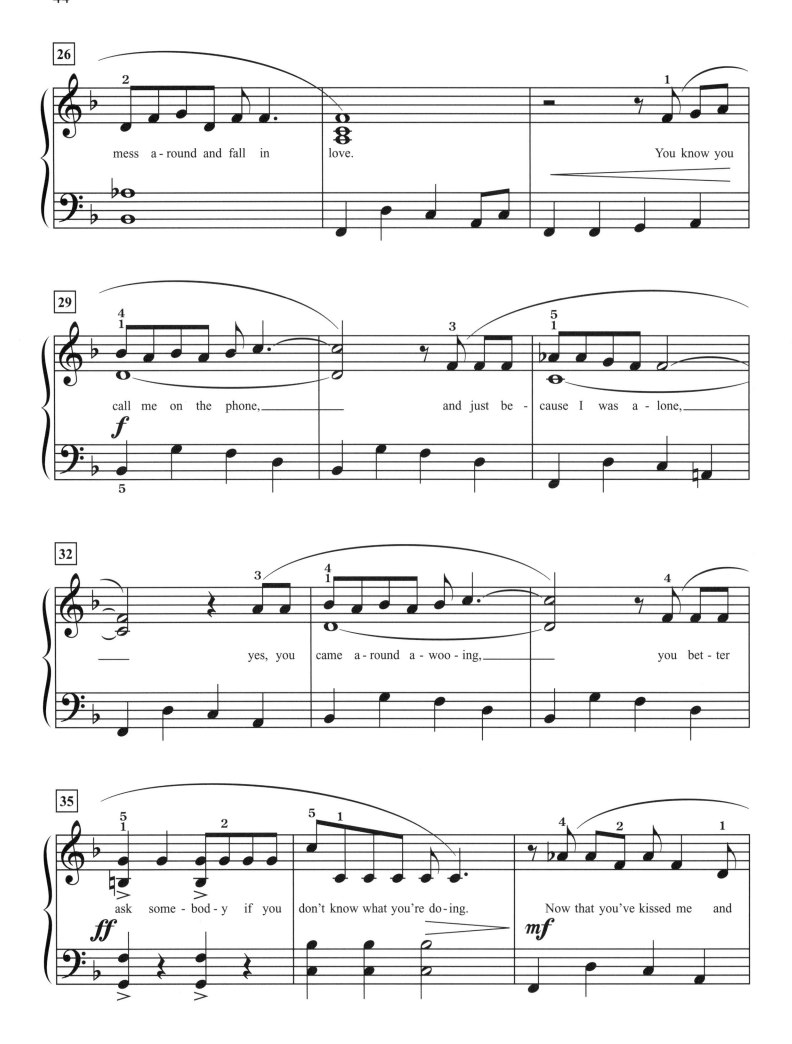

See You in September

Words by Sid Wayne
Music by Sherman Edwards
Arranged by Dan Coates

Moderately slow

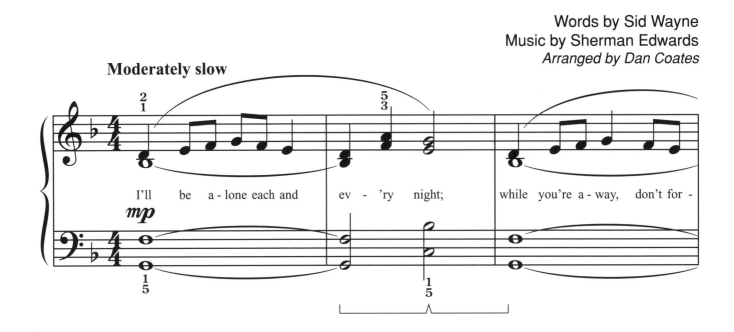

I'll be a - lone each and ev - 'ry night; while you're a - way, don't for -

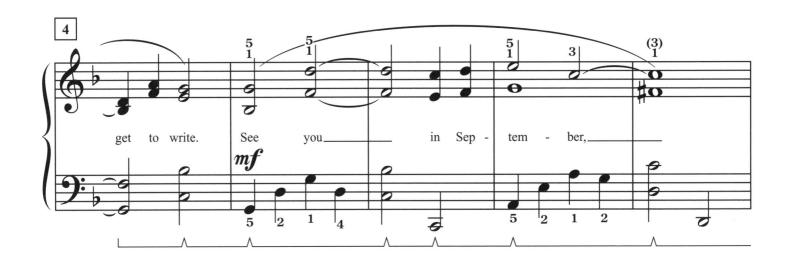

get to write. See you in Sep - tem - ber,

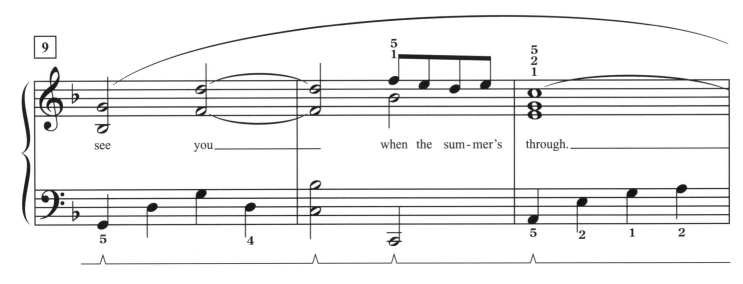

see you when the sum - mer's through.

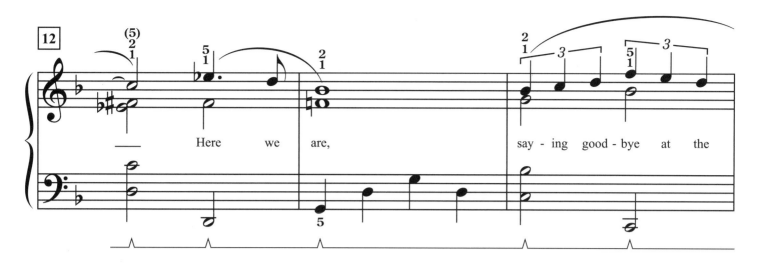

Here we are, say - ing good - bye at the

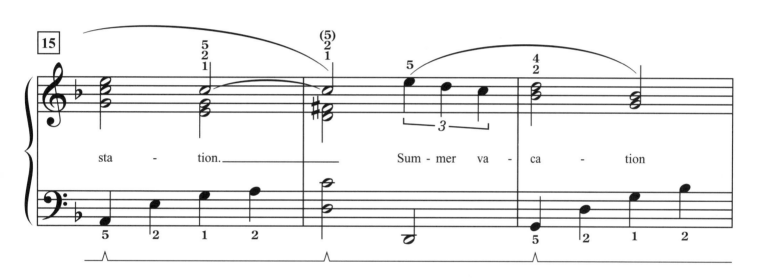

sta - tion. Sum - mer va - ca - tion

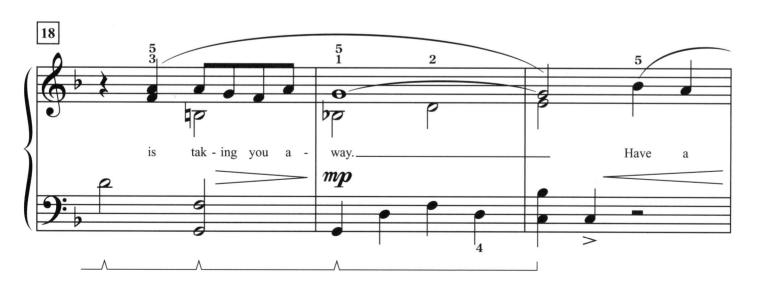

is tak - ing you a - way. Have a

good time,_____ but re- mem - ber_____ there is dan - ger

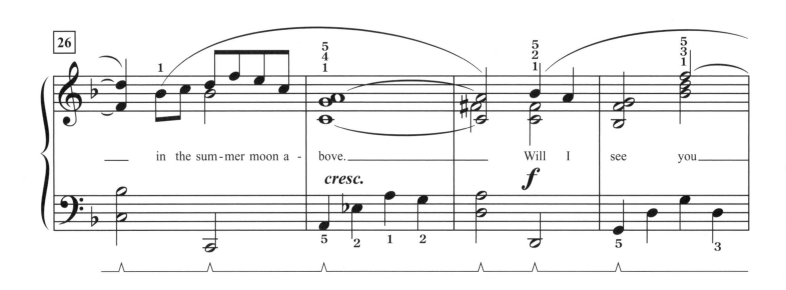

____ in the sum-mer moon a - bove._____ Will I see you____

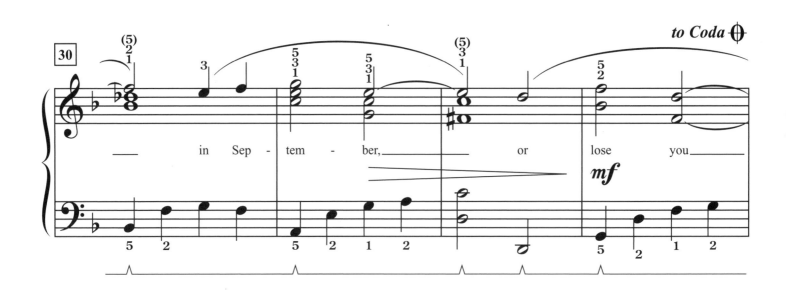

to Coda ⊕

____ in Sep - tem - ber,_____ or lose you____

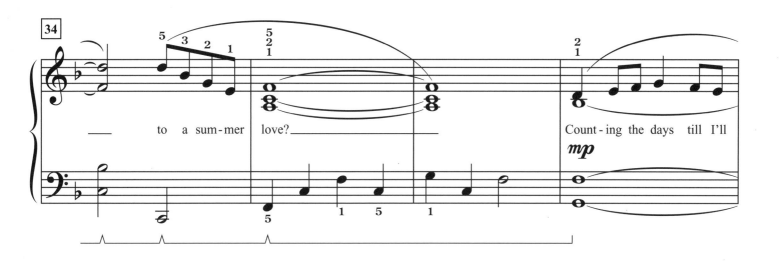

to a sum-mer love? _____ Count - ing the days till I'll

D.S. al Coda

be with you. Count - ing the hours and the min - utes, too. Have a

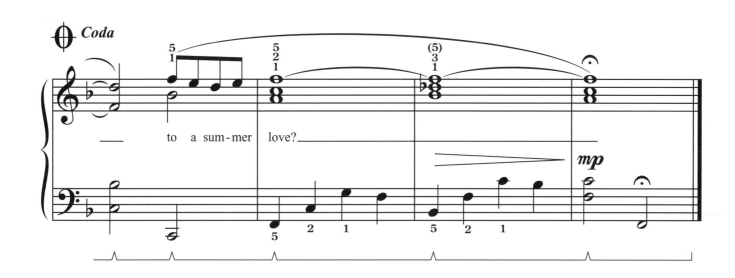

Coda

to a sum-mer love? _____

Sh-Boom
(Life Could Be a Dream)

Words and Music by
James Keyes, Carl Feaster, Floyd McRae,
Claude Feaster and James Edwards
Arranged by Dan Coates

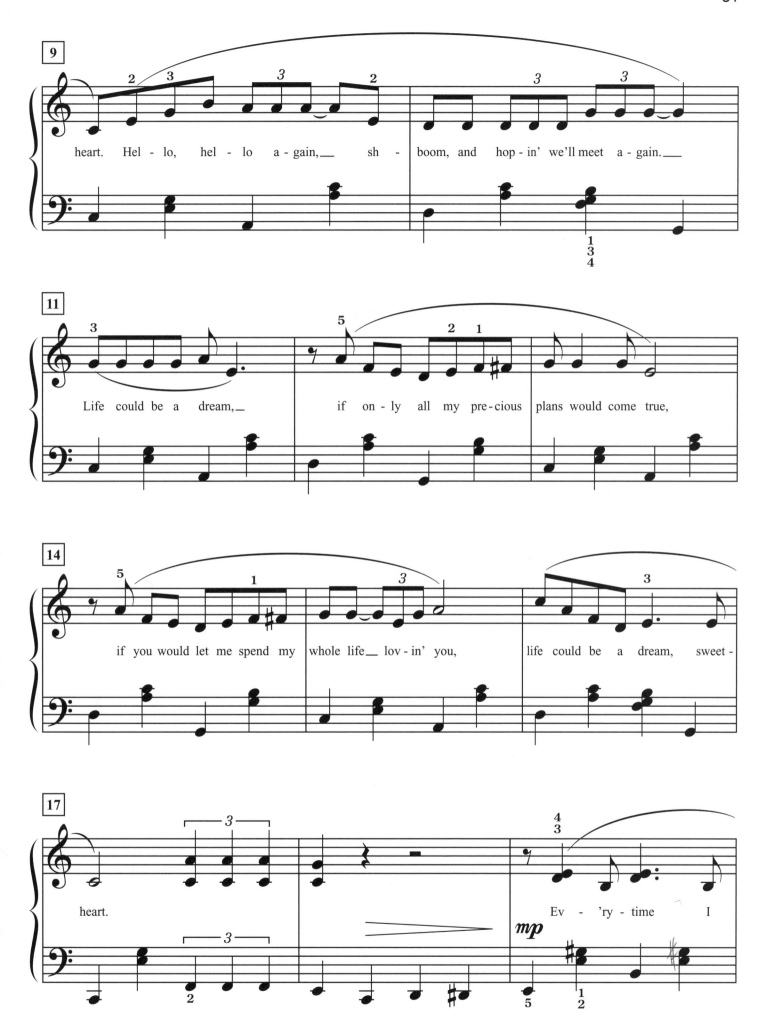

Shake Rattle and Roll

Words and Music by Charles E. Calhoun
Arranged by Dan Coates

30

hair done up so right,

wear-in' those dress-es, your

34

hair done up so right.

You look so warm, but your

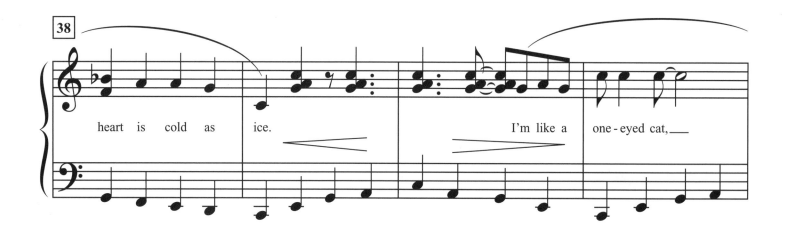

38

heart is cold as ice.

I'm like a one-eyed cat,___

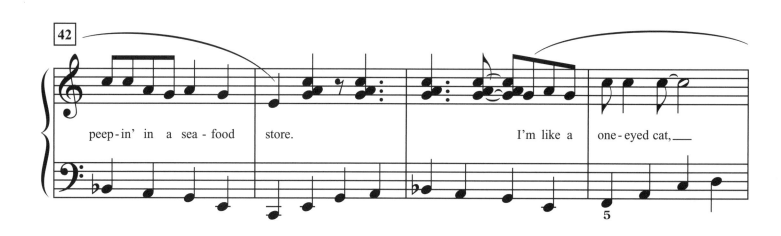

42

peep-in' in a sea-food store.

I'm like a one-eyed cat,___

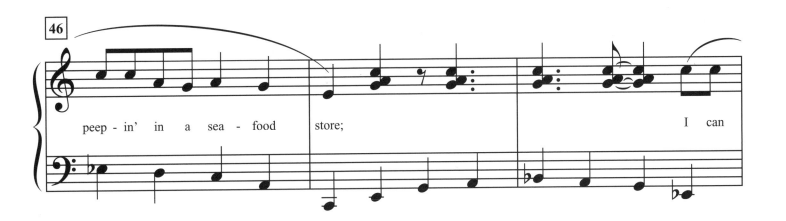

46 peep - in' in a sea - food store; I can

D.S. al Coda

49 look at you,___ tell you don't love me no more.

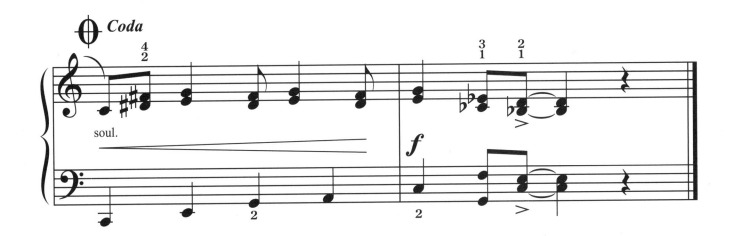

Coda

soul.

f

Verse 4:
I believe you're doin' me wrong
And now I know;
I believe you're doin' me wrong
And now I know.
The more I work,
The faster my money goes.

Peter Gunn

Music by Henry Mancini
Arranged by Dan Coates

With a steady, driving beat

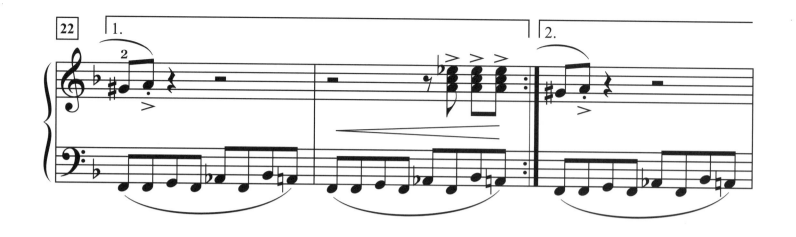

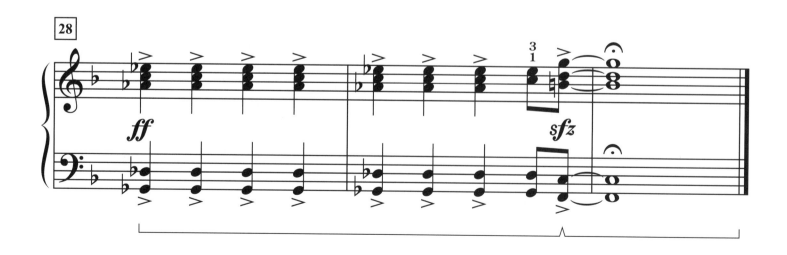

Sixteen Candles

Words and Music by
Luther Dixon and Allyson Khent
Arranged by Dan Coates

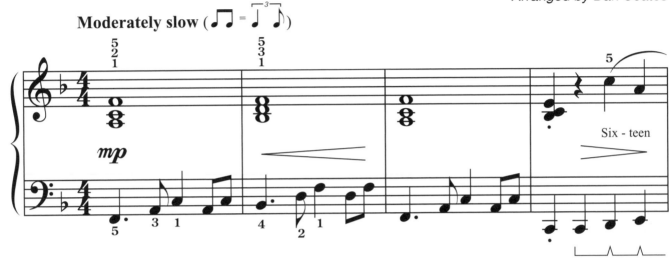

Splish Splash

Words and Music by
Bobby Darin and Jean Murray
Arranged by Dan Coates

Moderately, with a steady beat

Summertime Blues

Words and Music by
Eddie Cochran and Jerry Capehart
Arranged by Dan Coates

Steady, with a rock beat

LH *detached*

I'm a - gon - na raise a fuss, I'm a - gon - na raise a hol - ler,

a - bout a - work - in' all sum - mer just to

Well, I   did-n't go to work,   told the
Well, I   called   my   con-gress-man and

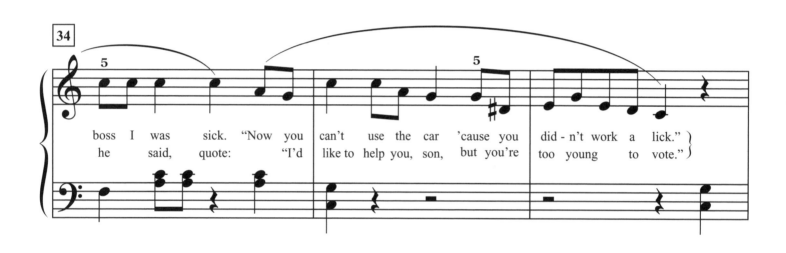

boss I was   sick.   "Now you   can't   use the car   'cause you   did-n't work a   lick."
he   said,   quote: "I'd   like to help you, son,   but you're   too young   to vote."

Some-times   I won-der   what   I'm a-gon-na do,   but there   ain't   no   cure   for the

cresc.

f

sum - mer - time —— blues.

I'm gon - na

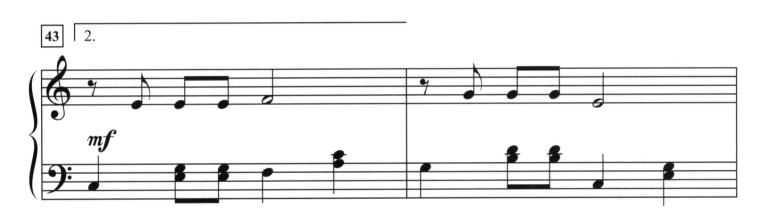

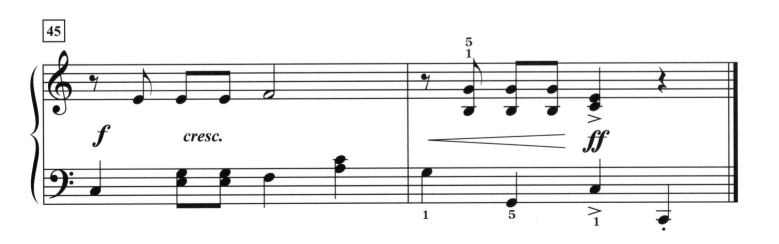

A Teenager In Love

Words by Doc Pomus
Music by Mort Shuman
Arranged by Dan Coates

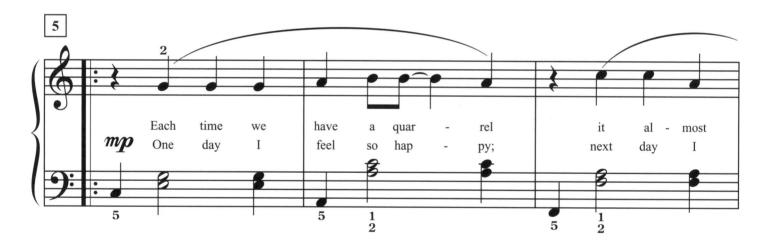

Each time we have a quar - rel   it al - most
One day I feel so hap - py;   next day I

breaks my heart,____   'cause I am so a - fraid____
feel so sad.____   I guess I'll learn to take____

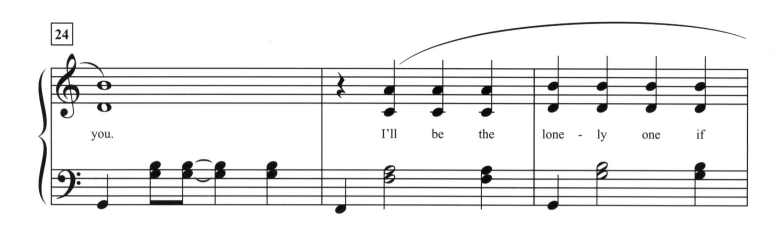

you.

I'll be the lone - ly one if

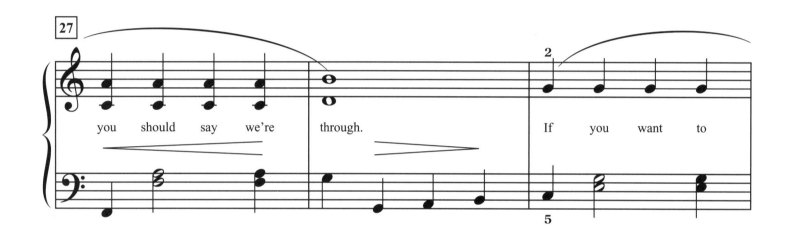

you should say we're through.

If you want to

make me cry,____ that won't be so hard to do.____

And if you should say good-bye,____ I'll still go on

What'd I Say

Words and Music by Ray Charles
Arranged by Dan Coates

Hey, ma - ma, don't you treat me wrong.— Come and love your dad - dy
See the girl with the dia - mond ring?— She knows how to
When you see me in mis - er - y,— come on, ba - by,

all night long.—
shake that thing.— All— right.
see 'bout me.—

See the girl with the red dress on?— She can do the Bird

all night long.— Oh,— yeah.

Tell me, what'd I say?—